Purchased from
Multnomah County
Title Wave Used
216 NE Knott St
503-9

Search
BOOKS

What
Is Digital
Citizenship?

Digital Safety Smarts

Preventing Cyberbullying

Mary Lindeen

Lerner Publications ◆ Minneapolis

To my parents, who taught
me that choosing to be kind
is always the best choice

Copyright © 2016 by Lerner Publishing Group, Inc.

All rights reserved. International copyright secured. No part of this book may be
reproduced, stored in a retrieval system, or transmitted in any form or by any means—
electronic, mechanical, photocopying, recording, or otherwise—without the prior written
permission of Lerner Publishing Group, Inc., except for the inclusion of brief quotations in
an acknowledged review.

Lerner Publications Company
A division of Lerner Publishing Group, Inc.
241 First Avenue North
Minneapolis, MN 55401 USA

For reading levels and more information, look up this title
at www.lernerbooks.com.

Library of Congress Cataloging-in-Publication Data

Lindeen, Mary.
    Digital safety smarts : preventing cyberbullying / by Mary Lindeen.
        pages cm. — (Searchlight Books™ — What Is Digital Citizenship?)
    Audience: Grade 4 to 6.
    Includes bibliographical references and index.
    ISBN 978-1-4677-9488-6 (lb : alk. paper)
    ISBN 978-1-4677-9691-0 (pb : alk. paper)
    ISBN 978-1-4677-9692-7 (eb pdf)
    1. Cyberbullying—Juvenile literature. 2. Cyberbullying—Prevention—
Juvenile literature. I. Title.
HV6773.15.C92L56 2016
302.34'302854678—dc23   2015016460

Manufactured in the United States of America
1 – VP – 12/31/15

Contents

Chapter 1

WHAT IS CYBERBULLYING?

Imagine this: You're in the school lunchroom eating with friends. Someone just told a funny joke. You and your friends are laughing. Then someone else from your class walks by. He reaches out and knocks over your milk carton. He laughs at you hysterically.

Bullying often happens when adults aren't around. What do you call bullying that happens online?

You are covered with milk. You are embarrassed. And this happens almost every day. This is an example of bullying.

Now imagine this: You get home after school and find that someone has sent you dozens of nasty e-mails. The sender has called you names. The sender has even threatened to hurt you. The e-mails also include links to embarrassing pictures that the sender posted of you. You feel awful. And this happens almost every day. This is an example of bullying too. It's called cyberbullying. Cyberbullying is any bullying that happens online.

Cyberbullying can make victims feel afraid to go online.

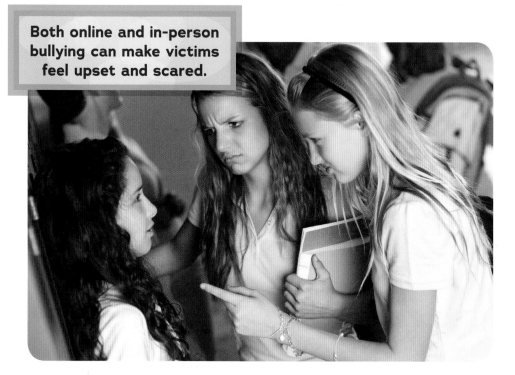

Both online and in-person bullying can make victims feel upset and scared.

Cyberbullying has much in common with face-to-face bullying. In both cases, one kid or a group of kids tries to make another kid feel embarrassed, weak, or afraid. Both kinds of bullying can include things like destroying someone else's property or making threats of violence.

When someone bullies you in person, she might take your backpack. When someone bullies you online, he might send a virus to attack your computer—or fill your e-mail inbox with hundreds of threatening messages.

Did You Know?

Adults can be victims of cyberbullying too. Police often use the word *cyberharassment* to describe threatening online behavior when it happens between adults. Whether the victim is a child or an adult, cyberbullying is never okay. Any online harassment needs to be taken very seriously.

Adults sometimes also face threatening online behavior.

Recognizing Cyberbullying

What are some other ways that people might cyberbully others? It can help to have some examples so you know cyberbullying when you see it.

One way is to exclude others from online activities or conversations. A cyberbullying victim might be blocked from an online group. Another way is to try to get you in trouble for something you didn't do. Someone might post embarrassing or hateful things on a website or blog. Then that person might sign those comments using your name. People reading the comments will think you wrote those things.

If someone posts something hateful under your name, you could get in trouble for something you didn't do.

Still another form of cyberbullying is to spread online rumors. Someone might text all her friends saying that a certain kid in your grade is changing schools because he gets teased. Even if the real reason he's changing schools is that his mom got a new job, now everyone thinks he's leaving because of teasing. The rumor sparks bullying both online and in person, making school hard for the boy.

ONE INSTANCE OF BULLYING CAN SOMETIMES LEAD TO MORE BULLYING.

Cyberbullying affects kids of many interests and backgrounds. You can't tell who might have been cyberbullied.

Victims of Cyberbullying

All kinds of kids are cyberbullied. Some victims are quiet and keep to themselves. Others are more talkative and outgoing. Some victims are popular and always seem to be surrounded by classmates. Others may prefer to have a smaller group of friends.

No matter what cyberbullying victims are like, one thing is true of them all: They do not deserve to be bullied. No one ever deserves to be frightened, hurt, or threatened by someone else, whether online or in person. Being a victim of cyberbullying is never anyone's fault. Everyone has the right to feel safe, both online and off.

Every kid deserves to feel happy and safe.

Chapter 2

WHY DOES CYBERBULLYING HAPPEN?

What makes a kid cyberbully someone else? There's no single reason why cyberbullying takes place. But more than half of those who cyberbully have been victims of bullying themselves.

Some have been bullied at school. Some have learned threatening behavior at home. They may be bullied by a parent, a sibling, or another family member.

Kids who grow up in homes where conflict is common are more likely to bully. How can reporting bullying help these kids?

Did You Know?

If someone is cyberbullying someone else, it can be a sign that he or she has emotional problems and needs to get help. Counselors and other trained adults can provide this help. Kids who report cyberbullying to an adult help both the victim and the person who is doing the bullying.

Counselors can help kids who bully learn to deal with their emotions.

IT CAN BE HARD TO UNDERSTAND WHY
ONE KID WOULD BULLY ANOTHER.
BUT THERE ARE MANY REASONS WHY
CYBERBULLYING TAKES PLACE.

Four Reasons for Cyberbullying

While there's no simple explanation for why cyberbullying happens, most cyberbullying occurs for one of four main reasons. Sometimes, a combination of these reasons is to blame.

The first reason is that the person behind the cyberbullying thinks her victim deserves it. She thinks her victim has done something wrong. She wants to teach that person a lesson. In this case, the one doing the bullying sees herself not as a bully but as a protector.

Some kids who bully do so to try to teach another kid a lesson.

The second reason is that the one doing the bullying feels powerless. Bullying makes him feel powerful. He likes feeling as if he can use technology to control others.

Cyberbullying can give people who lack power a way to feel more in control.

The third reason comes from peer pressure. Someone who bullies due to peer pressure might have friends who tease others for fun. She joins in the teasing to be accepted. Those who bully because of peer pressure often feel they have no power, just like those who bully to look tough.

Sometimes kids feel insecure. They may bully to try to feel like they belong.

The fourth reason behind bullying is that some kids don't realize they are bullying. They might simply be making nasty comments in response to mean messages they have received themselves. Or they might think it is fun to pretend to be tougher online than they are in real life. They might even just be kidding around. They do not see that their words and actions may hurt others.

Sometimes kids don't even realize that something they posted may hurt someone else.

Jealousy or hurt feelings can sometimes lead to bullying.

Close to Home

Most cyberbullying takes place between kids who know one another. Sometimes they are in the same school or class. Sometimes the person doing the bullying is even a friend of the victim. In these cases, the kid who bullies is often jealous of the friend or was hurt by something that happened in the relationship. Since cyberbullying is often anonymous, the victim doesn't always know it is a friend who is doing the bullying.

Both boys and girls can be victims of cyberbullying. Both can also be the ones who do the bullying. Boys are more likely to send messages that threaten to hurt another person. Girls are more likely to spread rumors, tell secrets, or make fun of or exclude others.

BOYS AND GIRLS CAN BOTH BE ON EITHER THE SENDING OR RECEIVING END OF CYBERBULLYING.

Chapter 3

THE EFFECTS OF CYBERBULLYING

Being bullied in person and online can have many of the same effects on the victims. They often feel extremely sad. Some of them fear facing another day. They do not feel good about themselves.

Bullying can have many bad effects. What is one harmful effect of bullying?

Sometimes the effects of cyberbullying can be even worse than the effects of in-person bullying. Kids who are being cyberbullied face pressures that kids who are being bullied in person do not. Kids who bully at school can hurt you only when they can see you. But someone who cyberbullies can find you no matter where you are. You can get a message from that person at school, at home, at a friend's home, or any place you're using technology.

Cyberbullying sometimes feels impossible to escape. It can happen anywhere technology is present.

TECHNOLOGY IS AN IMPORTANT PART OF
DAILY LIFE FOR MOST PEOPLE.

What's more, there's no real way to get away from
cyberbullying. The only way to avoid it is to go off-line
entirely. But most kids need to use technology for school.
Many also use it to have fun and connect with friends.

Anonymous and Always On

Another tricky thing about cyberbullying is that it's often anonymous. So those who bully online have little fear of being caught. In contrast, those who bully others in person usually are known to the victim. Others may see the bullying and try to stop it.

People may be around to see in-person teasing or bullying, but cyberbullying often has no witnesses.

Cyberbullying can also happen at any time of the day or night. Victims never know when the next message will come, so they may never feel safe. And they don't know how many messages they will get. Many messages can be sent very quickly to a lot of people. Someone who cyberbullies can post an embarrassing picture of the victim online or create a website aimed at embarrassing the victim. Everyone in the victim's family, school, and neighborhood can see the posts. So can millions of other people around the world.

Cyberbullying victims may not feel safe in their own homes.

Facing cyberbullying can make it hard to focus in school.

Mind and Body

Kids who are being cyberbullied often feel so bad that they have a hard time focusing in school. They might even be afraid to go to school. Their schoolwork may suffer. Their grades may go down. Some drop out of school completely. Others become angry and hostile. They might even become violent toward other students. Reacting to cyberbullying by bullying others is common.

Depression is another common effect of cyberbullying. Victims may feel sad and lonely. They don't trust people, and they don't feel safe. They might have a hard time sleeping. They might not feel like eating well or at all. They might use alcohol or drugs to try to make their sad feelings go away. Cyberbullying can affect the physical health of its victims as well as their emotional health.

VICTIMS OF CYBERBULLYING MAY FEEL SAD AND HOPELESS.

Chapter 4

WHAT YOU CAN DO ABOUT CYBERBULLYING

Most people know that cyberbullying is a serious problem. But it can be harder to know what to do if it happens. Having a plan in mind can help if cyberbullying is or ever becomes an issue for you or for someone you know.

Being prepared can help you face tricky online problems. What is one thing you can do to deal with cyberbullying if it occurs?

A Plan for Dealing with Cyberbullying

Do not respond. If you respond to cyberbullying, it will not make the bullying stop. It will only signal to the person doing the bullying that they've succeeded in making you upset or angry. Replying will encourage the person to keep attacking.

Keep records. Gather proof of the cyberbullying. Take pictures of what is on your screen. Print out messages you receive. Get physical proof that someone has targeted you.

Ask for help. Tell someone you trust, such as a family member, a teacher, or a good friend. Report the bullying to your school. No one ever has to deal with cyberbullying alone. Get support from people who care.

Telling a trusted friend or adult is important if you are facing cyberbullying.

Internet Safety

There are ways to use the Internet that can help stop cyberbullying before it starts. First, always be respectful and careful when you post anything online. Remember that everything you write or share online can be seen by others. Someone could use it against you in a cyberbullying attack. It could also be online forever. It might not embarrass you now, but in a few years, you could feel differently.

Something you post online may seem funny to you now, but you may regret posting it later.

Never share your passwords with anyone other than parents and teachers. And share your e-mail address and other personal information only with those you're sure you can trust. If you don't already know, find out how to use privacy settings and blocking features by doing an Internet search or asking your school's technology specialist.

Keep your passwords private.

Against the Law

The law can also help in the fight against cyberbullying. Many cities and states have laws about online bullying. These laws describe the behaviors that are considered cyberbullying.

LAW ENFORCEMENT OFFICERS TAKE CYBERBULLYING SERIOUSLY. THEY CAN HELP YOU IF YOU FEEL SCARED OR THREATENED BY SOMEONE ELSE'S BEHAVIOR.

Many cyberbullying laws include instructions for officially reporting and investigating cyberbullying. And they explain what should happen to kids who are caught cyberbullying. This could include reporting the behavior to a parent or a guardian. It could mean removing the kids from their schools or families for counseling and treatment.

Getting proper treatment is important for kids who struggle with anger and other feelings.

Take It Down

Companies that have websites or provide cell phone or other online services often offer tools for dealing with cyberbullying too. They want to protect their customers. Many cell phone services have call centers for reporting harassing phone calls or text messages.

> Customers can often call their cell phone companies to report bullying phone calls or texts.

Many social networking and online video sites also have reporting features. A user can alert the host company when inappropriate things are posted. Usually the company will start by looking into the report. Then it will remove anything from the site that breaks the rules.

Tell a company if you see something inappropriate posted on its site. An adult can help you report what you saw.

Be a Good Digital Citizen

Remember, if you are facing cyberbullying, there are many steps that you can take to deal with it. Lots of people and tools are available to help you. You can also tackle cyberbullying head-on by becoming part of the solution. Next time you go online, commit to posting only kind words. If you know of someone who's being cyberbullied, offer your support.

Cyberbullying is a difficult problem. But by using anti-bullying resources and reaching out to others, you can help to solve it. Take a stand today against cyberbullying. There's no better way to be a good digital citizen.

Be a good citizen, both online and off.

Technology and the Digital Citizen

Software developers, police, and cyberbullying victims alike have found a great tool to use in their quest to end cyberbullying: technology! Here are just a few of the programs and features they rely on to help stop online harassment.

Screen shots. A screen shot is a picture taken by a computer of the images shown on the screen. You can usually take a screen shot by pressing a certain combination of keyboard keys. Screen shots can capture threatening messages and serve as evidence when someone has been bullied.

Anti-bullying apps. An app is a program that can be installed on a cell phone or a tablet. Most anti-bullying apps work by sending a message to a parent's phone when their child's phone receives a text that contains bullying words. One app also has a panic button users can press to alert the police if a text is particularly frightening.

Spy-tracking software. Spy-tracking software can be installed on a computer or a cell phone. It can find out where anonymous messages are coming from. This way, police and cyberbullying victims can more easily figure out who is behind a cyberbullying attack.

Glossary

anonymous: not identified by name

blog: a website or web page that is usually run by one person and that contains personal writing, thoughts, and observations

counselor: a professional who is specially trained to give advice and to work with people who may be experiencing emotional problems

cyberbullying: when a child or a youth uses cell phones, computers, and other forms of technology to tease, frighten, or threaten someone else

cyberharassment: when an adult uses cell phones, computers, and other forms of technology to tease, frighten, or threaten someone else

depression: a medical condition in which a person feels very sad and hopeless

hostile: having or showing unfriendly feelings

rumor: information or a story that has been passed from person to person but has not been proven to be true

technology: machinery and equipment created by using scientific and engineering knowledge

victim: a person who has been harmed or injured by someone else

website: a location connected to the Internet that has one or more pages on the World Wide Web

LERNER

e

SOURCE

Expand learning beyond the printed book. Download free, complementary educational resources for this book from our website, www.lerneresource.com.

Learn More about Cyberbulling

Books

Donovan, Sandy. *How Can I Deal with Bullying? A Book about Respect.* Minneapolis: Lerner Publications, 2014. In this book of real-world questions and answers, readers learn more about why bullying happens and what they can do about it.

Golus, Carrie. *Take a Stand! What You Can Do about Bullying.* Minneapolis: Lerner Publications, 2009. In this title, readers discover why some kids bully and find out how to take a stand against them.

Nelson, Drew. *Dealing with Cyberbullies.* New York: Gareth Stevens, 2013. Nelson explains how to deal with cyberbullying and discusses the forms cyberbullying can take, along with guidelines for when to ask for help.

Websites

It's My Life
http://pbskids.org/itsmylife/friends/bullies
Check out this website to read about many different topics related to bullying.

KidsHealth
http://kidshealth.org/teen/expert/friends/expert_bullying.html
Get answers about what to do if you know someone who's being bullied—including what to do if you think the bullied person may harm himself or herself.

Stop Bullying
http://www.stopbullying.gov/kids/index.html
Visit this site to learn more about bullying of all kinds, including cyberbullying.

Index

Photo Acknowledgments

The images in this book are used with the permission of: © Yellow Dog Productions/The Image Bank/Getty Images, p. 4; © Peter Dazeley/The Image Bank/Getty Images, p. 5; © Steve Debenport/E+/Getty Images, p. 6; © JGI/Jamie Grill/Blend Images/Getty Images, p. 7; © Jay Newman/LWA/Blend Images/Getty Images, p. 8; © SolStock/E+/Getty Images, p. 9; © Kali Nine LLC/Vetta/Getty Images, p. 10; © Brand New Images/Taxi/Getty Images, p. 11; © SuperStock, p. 12; © Richard Clark/Photolibrary RM/Getty Images, p. 13; © sunabesyou/Shutterstock.com, p. 14; © Alexey Tkachenko/E+/Getty Images, p. 15; © Marcel ter Bekke/Flickr RF/Getty Images, p. 16; © fstop123/E+/Getty Images, p. 17; © Hung Chung Chih/Shutterstock.com, p. 18; © Altrendo/Getty Images, p. 19; © Cultura/Igore/Getty Images, p. 20; © MachineHeadz/E+/Getty Images, p. 21; © Tetra Images/Getty Images, p. 22; © Jochen Tack/Alamy, p. 23; © Chris Schmidt/E+/Getty Images, p. 24; © Brendan O'Sullivan/Photolibrary RM/Getty Images, p. 25; © PhotoAlto/SuperStock, p. 26; © Sofie Delauw/Cultura RF/Getty Images, p. 27; © PeopleImages.com/Digital Vision/Getty Images, p. 28; © Lewis J Merrim/Photo Researchers RM/Getty Images, p. 29; © iStockphoto.com/Alejandro Rivera, p. 30; © iStockphoto.com/scyther5, p. 31; © Richard Hutchings/CORBIS, p. 32; © BSIP/Universal Images Group/Getty Images, p. 33; © g215/Shutterstock.com, p. 34; © iStockphoto.com/PeopleImages, p. 35; © Chris Ryan/Compassionate Eye Foundation/Taxi/Getty Images, p. 36.

Front cover: © iStockphoto.com/Pamela Moore

Main body text set in Adrianna Regular 14/20
Typeface provided by Chank